# Love
## Unconditional

## Poetry to Heal

# Jennifer Hershelman

Love Unconditional

Poetry to Heal

Cover art by Jennifer Hershelman, 2023.

First edition.

Published by Four Wild Geese Design, Mount Shasta, California 96067

ISBN 978-1-7324373-7-1

## Dedication

My book is dedicated to my incredible friend
Brandon Cascia,
whose intense healing journey,
that I have had the honor to walk with him on
has shown me the true depth
of the human spirit!
He has been my inspiration
for many of my poems.
Thank you Brandon
I Love You

## Foreword

Love allows-
when your unhappy
I love us both enough
to give you your space.

Love is patient.

Love shines softly,
not blindingly, overbright.

Love does not compete,
become puffed up with pride
or need to win.

Love-
hears no evil
sees no evil
speaks no evil

Love believes the good
in all things.

Love is unconditional.

Cheryl Lunar Wind

# Preface

In our society, the true beauty and power
of unconditional love has been lost.

I have been blessed while living and healing
in Peru, I was able to experience the truth of
love. What it is, what it feels like and what it
really means to give love to yourself; how it
empowers you to be and live freely. It is the
energy necessary for us to heal, and be complete
as individuals and as community. First, we
must learn to understand it as a concept, an
energy, a feeling and a practice. Learning to
give it to ourselves first, and then to others.

*"Love is patient and kind. Love is not jealous or
boastful or proud or rude. It does not demand
its own way. It is not irritable, and it keeps no
record of being wronged. It does not rejoice
about injustice but rejoices whenever the truth
wins out. Love never gives up, never loses faith,
is always hopeful, and endures through every
circumstance."*
1 Corinthians 13:4-7 New Living Translation

Unconditional love is taking accountability for you,
and your actions, while doing so with kindness and compassion
for yourself.

# Contents

## Shadow

It's OK I love you
That time you lost your temper
and hurt the one you love
It's OK I love you

You're allowed to forgive
That thought you had
you feel is twisted and shouldn't exist
It's OK I love you

You're allowed to express
and untwist
It's OK I love you

You're allowed to exist
That urge you feel
to hate, to hurt, to rape, to rage
It's OK I love you

It's not wrong to be felt
It's OK I love you
Please don't give up on yourself
for in the depths of darkness
there is light to be found

It's OK I love you

Every piece has it's place
My heart will always have space
for all that you have to face
It's OK I love you

Those parts of you that are held in shadow are always the parts of you that need the most love and acceptance from you. They are the pieces that have been traumatized and beat down, while living in the matrix. By giving them unconditional self love you transmute and transform them, building yourself up, and bringing them back into balance with your heart.

"God, the Universe, Source, the Creator, Spirit are all one and the same—pure unconditional love. The more we learn to give unconditional love to ourselves the closer we are to Source." JH

# Worthy

People lost, thinking
worthiness is something that has to be attained
to be gained

Rolling on the ground thinking
they have to be trained

-Fetch,  Go get it
get the stick
get the job
get the money
get the car

Do it now. Do it right. Bring it back.
Prove your worth.

-people lost, believing the lie
Well, its time to be found
let the lie fall to the ground

You are worthy
by your very presence
your soul, your every essence
is essential and enough

Its time to let go
No more hoops
No more lies
See with unclouded eyes

You are worthy just by being
So, thank you for being

Judgments are just self-reflections of our parts that don't feel good enough or worthy. The matrix teaches us that to feel better about ourselves we have to judge and put others down. Instead we can build ourselves up. When you find yourself standing in judgment of someone else, take a deeper look, find the hurt, sad, angry, insecure, jealous part of yourself and show it love and compassion. Let your self judgments fall away, and allow yourself to see your worth. Know you are worthy, no matter what. When you are able to do that for yourself, you will be able to look at the world judgment free.

# Shatter

Awake---I lay
crushing weight enters my space
wrapping me in its dark embrace

Breathing
Wheezing
chest slowly squeezing

Sadness flowing
the pain seeps in

Shatter like glass
the universe of pain
holding your soul
crashes into me
fills my heart

I don't know where to start
Wish I could take it all away
But that's not my part to play
Test of faith

Will you ever feel safe
to let go

What can I do but hold space
Its not my place
My heart can barely keep pace
The pain seeps in--
Shatter

## Pure

I just want to love you
truly,
free and pure

I just want to flow
and see where we go

I want you to feel
free to be you

I want you to know I love
watching you grow

I hope that you heal
and know what is true

That I'll always love you
through and through

no matter what it is that
you choose to do

# Hello

Hello,
I'd like to greet the man
I've been forever waiting to meet

not afraid to stand in his power

working tirelessly every hour

letting the shadows fall away

learning to let true love come play

nothing will stand in his way

the truth will fill his eyes
washing away the lies
his knowing ever growing

his heart shines bright this day
showing him the way
on his path he'll never sway

I just wanted to say
I love you.

## Ancient

Singing to the tree--
the words, ancient and deep
from another time,
nearly forgotten, hidden, asleep.

Suddenly,
everything shifts, merges and converges.

Now,
I'm sitting in the tree,
feeling it become me.
When I open my eyes,
I'm touching the sky
The wind blowing through me as leaves on the tree
totally and utterly free.

I flow to the ground
traveling through roots
reaching out,
as far as the eye can see--
energy all connected, intertwined and integrated.

The black hills grass giggled and tickled above
as I flow through roots below.
I feel the wind again,

rustling and tussling
as the Buffalo I saw a mile back
now,
stands over and on me.
Grass is a hive mind,
each blade blows singularily and together.
They giggle harmoniously.
The wind tickled
as we giggled and waved
loving to be swayed.

For a brief moment,
I feel myself rise
and see through Buffalo eyes.

Then snap,
I'm back at the tree
feeling my body, all around me
my feet planted in dirt.
Standing in sunshine,
bees singing to me.

Now,
time to move along.
Nothing can go wrong.
Time to help people live,
pure, connected and free.

## Untitled

You say you love me
      you say you care
Yet as I sleep,
I feel
your energy creep
pushing your feelings over mine

A feeling so un-divine

I can hardly believe you think
      its fine

Thinking I should live your
will and not mine.

Truth be told,
I must be bold,
and your will,
will never hold the truth of my light.

# Love Is

Love is freedom
never pushing over me
only holding me steady,
as I tread these murky waters.
Gently lifting me when I feel down

Slowly caressing the fear and pain
till it loosens it's grip and leaves
my body

Love is Pure never telling me who to be
only showing me what I can be,
and how to get there

Love never pulls or pushes me
wanting me to feel low
to the ground

Love builds me up, wanting
me to be, all that I can be

Guiding me forward
shining a light so bright
all that is not right
for me dissolves away

# Need

Walking around feeling incomplete
creating the need to compete
crying and vying for attention
I must have more for my ascension--

The feeling of need turns to greed
feeling hungry,

I must feed--
Filler--
Bring the
--food
--drugs
--sex
--praise
Give it here, I want it now!

Filled to the brink of extinction--
how do we find true completion?

When we see that its not
you that I need but me

we will live in a world
full, happy and free

Needing someone creates attachments to them and gives your power away. You may like them, love them, care about them, but you sure as hell do not need them or anyone. You have everything you need already inside you. Looking for it from outside sources is what is keeping you from tapping into what you already have. Love those parts that feel that need, take your power back, tune into your heart and know that you are enough.

# Free

For all of the darkness
you say that is you

Your presence in life
lights up my day

For all of the parts you seem to hate
I see what it is that makes you great

Isn't it time to drop the weight
Love yourself and integrate

Let the world finally see
What it means to be you
when you are totally free

Now's the time,
the perfect hour
So, stand in your sovereign power

Shine your light bright
and never forget
that what's in your heart
the magic I see
can set the world free

# Just a Love Song for You

I love you
and I'm going to see this through

Cause Baby, There ain't nothing we can't do,
When we work together

And I see you, your beauty shining through

and all the work you do, to be honest, healed and true

I love you
And I know you feel it too
And I'm going to see this through
no matter
what I have to doooo

Youuuu amaze me
as much as you drive me crazy
and
I love you
No matter what
you have been through.

I love you
No matter what we have to go through
I love you
and I'm going to see this through

Cause Baby, There ain't nothing we can't do,
When we work together

And I see you, your beauty shining through
and all the work you do, to be honest, healed and true

I love you
And I know you feel it too
And I'm going to see this through
no matter
what I have to doooo

Youuuu amaze me
as much as you drive me crazy
and
I love you
No matter what
you have been through

I love you
No matter what we have to go through.

# Realizations

Cheryl Lunar Wind


Lessons---
I've learned that if I treat a person---a certain way
that I will be treated the same way---by someone else.


Its ok--I love you.*


Someone told me on my bday---
"Your not old--your experienced."
I feel sad that I am old--
If I knew then, what I do now---
Would I, could I have done more?
To be 'experienced' and have youth and joy--
wouldn't that be cool?


Another friend told me-- .
"Don't sing---your voice is flat."
I feel sad, I didn't do more with music and art---
Learn, Practice and Do--
I love singing,
and I will keep on.
I feel sad,
I never learned to play an instrument or draw a picture.


Its ok--I love you.

My creative successes were around---
Furnishing a house, Feeding a family on a budget.
My energy was spent--
raising kids
making ends meet.
That has been my whole life---
when married, I added the role of peacemaker.

So many lessons, so much sadness.
Its ok--I love you.

In the night, grief finds me.
I wanted to travel, give talks, hold workshops---
I was told 'Play in your own back yard'.

Its ok--I love you.

Now,
I do what I know--
I keep it simple--
I live in my own reality.
I give myself--
love and acceptance.
Its ok--I love you.

*J.H.

# Replenishing

Sitting silent in the woods
a gentle breeze brushes by your face
its not the wind
the trees are breathing all around you

Breathing life into the world,
        Replenishing

Standing, silently, crying against a trunk
-sweet release, ease the energy out

Trees

Soaking in your tears, your fears
Holding space for all your pain
with nothing to gain

But a song, of love and gratitude
        Replenishing
Necessary.

For the space they hold
for us all

Standing tall
beacons of energy

Anchoring in reality
Shifting the winds

Swirling the world
into
Peace and balance.

# Dance

When the earth was new
the plants had barely grown
no medicine was known

people needed healing

sisters sat in council
and felt into their hearts
where a primal energy swirled

just as the winds that cross
the plains, bringing in the rain

When they stood together and
stretched their bodies out
the Earth shifted beneath their feet

helping them to feel complete
as they continued stretching
and twirling in the dirt

their hearts overflowed
primal healing rushing
from head to toe

Each movement affecting a change
within the others...
with their hearts beating in harmony
their bodies moving to the rhythm

of their stomping feet, in sync
with the breath of the Earth

The clouds began to swim and shift
with them, the sisters
twist and flow
as rain poured down
the dirt turned to mud

the healing energy,
a giant wave--

Dance as a healing art
was born that day,
a sacred and ancient gift
from the spirits
that is most powerful
when it comes from the heart--
not to be misused to get your way
not to be abused, to lie, cheat and confuse.

It's time.
Come back to the start,
feel it from your heart,
time to hold space for
healing to take place.

# Friendship

Friendship is not a currency
used to get your way

My loyalty cannot be bought or bartered,
just because you say you'll stay

People are not things,
here to please you, to have, or to be given

Friends aren't friends
only when they do what you say

This is not a game
for you to play

Friendship is uplifting, kind
and caring

Daring to let you in, show you my heart
trusting you won't tear it apart

Friendship is supporting, respecting
each others boundaries and decisions

Hoping that we can learn and grow,
that I won't have to let you go.

## Reflections

As we wonder through this world,
Life lessons flow to us
through reflections.

Most only see an ugly seer--

~things that make us want to sneer
~things that we want to fear
~things that we can't stand to feel
~things that are there for us to heal

then moving on, rather quickly
don't want to stay and
keep looking sickly

not open to the other side
of the beauty that's inside
the strength and courage
that is there is
covered over by that fear

If we'd only stop and breathe
take it all in
and let ourselves see
the Beauty in me
is in you too

You have your own magic, beauty and talents. There is no need to compare yourself to others. The more you give yourself unconditional self-love, the more you step into your own beauty. So love yourself and own your magic!

# Mama Earth--Father Sky Meditation

Many of us did not receive unconditional love from our parents while growing up. Not knowing unconditional love themselves, they did the best they could. This meditation will help us to feel unconditional love from our divine parents.

We are going to take a moment to center ourselves.

Take 3 deep breaths,

Pulling your awareness into your heart space,
with each breath.

Now that you are centered in your heart, I want you
to focus on the feeling of love.
Allow it to fill your heart.

Next,
breathe in deeply
and as you breathe out-
send all that love down
to the center of Mama Earth.

When you breathe in
feel her love for you
coming back up into you.

Now, hold that energy,
love from Mama in your heart
along with your love.

Deep breathe in
and as you breathe out
send your love
up to Father Sky.

On your next breath in,
feel the love from Father Sky
flow down to you
through your crown, down your spine,
and into your heart.

Now hold all three energies in your heart,
the unconditional love from Mama Earth,
Father Sky and the love for yourself.

Swirl them together,
Breathe in, and on
your out breath
send all that love to your entire body,
let it fill you from head to toe.

# Fear

Fear makes everything
so unclear

the pages begin to tear

everything seems unfair

hatred and anger
flying everywhere

Does anyone even truely care?

There isn't enough so I won't share
Hey look, OMG is there something
over there?

I'm gonna loose everything I hold dear

What can I do? The end is near.

Stop, Breathe
Allow yourself to believe
You have the strength to face anything


Stop, Breathe
Allow yourself to feel
Love yourself so that you can heal

Fear exists for you to overcome it!
It's here to show you your true strength.
For once you face all your fears and
transmute them with love, there is
nothing that can stand in your way!

## Sacred

Insanity is here
everybody clinging to fear
nothing holds dear

The sacredness of life
lost in the fold

All the truths hidden
and untold
stories of old
of sacred rituals
and
Respect
all kept, swept
to the side
making it easier
to decide to hide
all that darkness up inside
Thinking you can stow it,
control it, avoid it, deny it.

Hold your breath, suck it in

until it leaks
it's tendrils begin
to peek out
wriggling and slithering about
touching all those you know,
friend or foe

Like a wildfire burning darkly through
the  forest
echoing your pain
like a chorus
till nothing lies left before us.

Take heart for
there is a way
to transform the darkness within.

It's a path not for
the faint of heart
very few truly wish
to take part.

For the light of the fire
burning in your heart
will tear all the lies apart,
rendering your defenses asunder
because your truth is
the true plunder.

Even if its
hard to bear
The more you allow yourself to sit and stare
The true vision you will share
and all the monsters slithering inside,
turn into little boys just trying to hide,
scared and hurt, lost in the pain
waiting for you
to truly see

they just need love
from you
to be free.

## Love Unconditional

The matrix has people
fooled to think
that love is weak

One of the ways
it keeps people asleep

People greatly underestimate
the strength it takes
to look at what--

The world deems as ugly
take it in your heart
and let the judgment fall apart

The determination that is needed
to feel all the pain and let it go
drain down into the earth to be healed

The magic that is necessary
to face your fears with love
and transmute them

The energy it takes
to stand tall
through all the
shame, blame and guilt
they try to bury you with

The bravery it takes
to speak up and say
Enough is Enough
I'm done playing "this" game

I Love Myself

Love Unconditional

Judgment, shame, blame, guilt and fault are all Bullshit energies that are used to keep you down. All humans make mistakes, we are meant to make mistakes, that is how we learn. We must learn not to hold ourselves down with shame and guilt, but stand tall with self love. Holding ourselves accountable and taking responsibility for our actions, all while building ourselves up so that we can learn to do better and be better for the next time.

"Wisdom is born from self-love." JH

# My Prayer

## My Wish

is for peace, love, balance,

freedom and unhindered healing for all;

the land, the water, the spirits,

all beings and people.

Thank-You

author-

Jennifer is most at home in the mountain areas.
She currently resides in the Mount Shasta area
with her cat Pina. She has traveled the world,
connecting with the heart and spirit of Gaia. Her
healing journey has been long and intense. Now
she shares wisdom she has gained along the way.
Love Unconditional is her first published book.

Made in the USA
Columbia, SC
30 September 2023

23556431R00031